ELIZABETHAN

VIII

JONATHAN LOVEJOY

ELIZABETHAN

The Complete Poems of Elizabeth Peele

Volume VIII

Armageddon Publishing

Cover: *Lost Pleiad,* 1884
William Adolphe Bouguereau (1825-1905)

ISBN-10: 0692319255
ISBN-13: 978-0692319253

For every Elizabeth

Introduction

Carmen Angelina Coletti (Elizabeth Peele) was perhaps the greatest composer who ever lived. After her death, studies of her music revealed a body of work—almost exclusively instrumental—of such beauty and power as to defy description. Even so, her lifelong reclusiveness rendered them obsolete to the world, and these musical treasures may remain apart from public view forever.

Even those few who heard her original scores did so in quiet apprehension, that this beautiful widow—lost somewhere deep in North Carolina farming country—brought forth music as completely ingenious as any ever written before. The sounds of greatness flowing from this woman's piano, surely this is not meant to be! For what purpose can she truly serve as a neoclassical composer in a jaded modern world, except as a curiosity and eventually, a fountain of eternal exploitation?

But while music did serve as a profession for her since she was twelve—her only wage being a sound mind and spirit—there was still another expression, both private and unintentional, equally meant for her eyes only. Gathered posthumously, so few of these "assemblies" can be called unique or special, and likely cannot set her apart from any other lonely poet in the world. But still they live on, as a glimpse into the mind of a musical genius and abused woman of Faith. Written parallel to her music over the years—with no striving for greatness or immortality—these poetic trifles, ironically, may be the only compositions of hers the world will ever hear.

Elizabethan

or

"The Assemblies"

Volume VIII

Such is the grandest music among us—

Poets…

Such are the wildest thoughts among us—

Composers…

The Book of Vera

228th Assembly

1049

In the event of nuclear holocaust
Shelter would be found
Preference—beneath the earth
In the solemn ground

The rounded column of dirt above
Is thy burial mound

1050

"Beauty is as beauty does," I hear
Some are known to say
Angels to help ease the pain
Of living another day

The ancestry rolls along in tune
Whose apt to carry on
The wind speaks a neverending voice
To bid my soul "goodbye"

From 1823, harmonies play
The voice of *Semiramide*
Lightning from the Coletti pen
Strikes the modern day

1051

I wanted to live
I wanted to be happy
But God sent the Devil to me,
And he said—

You flat fluck—yours is a prison
Above ground
Until I have your body
Rotting beneath the earth

Below ground

1052

There's a work that calls every day
The simple art of composing a poem
Is not lost—
On those who wish to have it

229th Assembly

1053

Try hard to pluck a tree
After its roots have grown

You're always going to pay—
For comparison and contrast
Give the tree time to grow
The roots will find their way
Growing down into the ground so deep

As to defy logic

1054

They were victims of circumstance
Excuse for hiding in
Violence spewed on one another
The kitchen—and the den

Three sisters and their mother
Gathering once again

1055

At the base of Mt. St. Helens
Politics engenders hate
On the eve of eschatology
Beyond the modern gate

Church cults rise and fall
Who profess to know the Spirit
Having a form of Godliness
But none the power thereof

At the foot of the snowy mountain
Rumblings sway the trees
On the eve of Armageddon
Before the fire glows again

Fools dance their lives away
Igniting lust and sin
On the eve of eschatology
Before the mountain blows again

1056

Attempts to make peace will fail
At the carnival of violence
When tempers have flared and gone
Devastation remains to be seen

At the carcass of a mule
The storm of violence will rise
Raging in the hearts of enemies
Who were friends once before

230th Assembly

1057

On the scales of life
Are written notes of truth
Up and down the length of it
For all the world to hear

Listen to the scales of truth
As the notes of life are played
They sing truth for your ears only
That should never be spoken to another

1058

I see her departing in the white chariot
Truth laced uncertainties anew
Eternal truth is in the air
That which we dare not face

Though I stroll the grounds of adult life
They are laughing at me again
Though my self-esteem tries to build
It is not able

Because of the voice of other people—
Laughing at me again

1059

I would like to have 22 affairs
The woman said to him
Spoken without compromise
And then she buried him

At the grave, another woman said
You're holding up so well
Then she kissed her lover on the cheek
Enchanted by her spell

1060

Above the Lake of Good Intentions
A white funnel appears
Given substance by the water alone
Reaching toward the sky

The water cloud spins in power
Across the waters of the lake
Churning it into a rolling sea
Of roaring, splashing waves

The water spout declines its power
Inclined to go away
Calming the waters of the lake
Beneath a portrait in gray

231st Assembly

1061

Evil comes disguised in beauty
So goes the busy Bee
Lovely green of the Ivy Leaf
Poison to you and me

1062

I am dead to the world

As it is of me

Hardly was a kindness

Unlaced in venom

My wish to live among them

A faded autumn leaf

1063

Surrounded by none who care
For artistic concern
From the wise down to the simple
A disinterested burn

Pieces of the puzzle—poorly placed
By those who claim to know
Without breath, the body dies
Verses have to breathe

Cast no pearl before a swine
Where it is trampled or eaten
Again, without breath to breathe
Verses die

1064

Blazing high into the sky
A daredevil rocket ship
Genius from father to son—
Forgotten

232nd Assembly

1065

My direction is not to entertain
But to delight, horrify, mystify
And testify
To the Glory of the coming of the Lord

In hopes to transmogrify
While I put my foot up Satan's
Ascrack-o-lantern
And kick him to the Moon

1066

In the amaranthine station
I gather with my hand
Watching everything I touch
Dry up and turn to sand

I move up to the counter
Knowing I have to pay
Too weak to gather the money I need
To make it go away

The attendant said "hurry up!"
Humiliation mode
I'm sorry for the delay, I say
My mind is on the road

1067

Inside the palace of lost dreams
I sought until I found
But when I fought to gather hope
It crumbled to the ground

Even though I smiled a greeting
To everyone I saw
Their laughter was at my expense
To crush my soul to straw

I gathered hope the best I could
What price I had to pay
Trying to make it back to Life
'Fore it was gone away

1068

I'm going to die within the year
'Tis my daily refrain
Spoken by the voice of history
With only truth to gain

233rd Assembly

1069

Sincere effort is no substitute
For preparation and ability
So goes the journey through the swamp
Where possibility goes to die

Bid no concern to readiness
In the divine Will of God
Fate is thine preparation
Destiny is thine ability

1070

Soon we shall sleep—
Waiting to be changed
In the twinkling of an eye
Before the Great and Terrible Day
Of the Lord come

Buildings sway—
Threatening to fall
While the Earth is under Fall of Night
But in the Midst of Chaos—there is hope
Brought upon the world once a year
A story told by the light of a single Star
In the melodies of Crimson and White

Children sway—
Poised on the edge of a fall
A tumble into the abyss of sorrow
And moral turpitude
Immoral servitude
To the philosophy of the last day
Which is blood, money, fear—
And death

While people scurry—
Through the night city
On the edge of the eschatology scream
Some look to the Blessed Hope
The fearful escape from bondage
Which is the knowledge that soon—
We shall sleep—
To escape the Great and Terrible day—
Before the coming of the Lord

1071

On the death of my blue flower
No fragrancy in bloom
Azure petals—wither and die
In my grieving room

1072

Humans attack like dogs
In residence—
Or in the learning halls

Hey, Mr. Sunshine—
Mr. Tamborine Man
What the devil is your plan?

234th Assembly

1073

New Orleans was every bit as scared

As Sodom and Gomorrah

The splintering of the big easy

A warning of things to come

1074

Where the roaming dead go to sleep
Lies a burial urn
Looted by loved ones of the deceased
Lessons too late to learn

Doors rattle on their hinges
Cold spots--an icy chill
Forboding falls with the nightime
Eyes at the windowsill

1075

The evening day is deep twilight
Nearby the edge of night
Shadows recall fair death of light
Beyond their feeble sight

1076

Rossini is Mozart unrestrained
Inspired melody preordained
Harmony from the sky

Resounding the Great Music Hall
Operatic by no thought at all
On genius, they rely!

235th Assembly

1077

A prairie flower blooms at night
In the autumn of the leaves
She labours to my soul's delight
At the harvest of the sheeves

Close even when we're far apart
In prayer to what she believed
Her life was for my grieving heart
And every joy it received

My spirit calls for "Caroline"
A memory doth achieve
Her soul in paradise divine
At her bedside to bereave

As I lay down my life and worth
My suffering will alleve
Our bodies lie beneath the earth
Reunited in reprieve

1078

In the grass is a swarm of bees
Waiting outside my door
Iconoclast the least of these
Sunday at Yom Kippur

Thirty nine days of punishment
All of them undeserved
From home to the halls of learning
Trouble at every turn

Iconic blasts arc cumbcrsomc
Running the lawn of bees
With pearls lined in a teaching row
To learn as the elite

1079

When Satan stands outside the door
Do not let him in
Disguised as though he means no harm
With malice for all men

1080

I know as surely as I live
I can never go home again
That path is overgrown with thistles
As prickly as a pin

The house they built for me is fear
My excuse for hiding in

1081

Like the chiming of the whistle train
Swiss colony days do beckon
A calling in the Autumn Wind
Beneath the Harvest Moon

Over golden fields of prosperity
Better days extend their hand
Through the wilderness where I walk alone
Across the grieving land

236th Assembly

1082

I have no knowledge where to go
But still I travel on
Across the ocean-- "where to fore"
Elizabethan dawn

None the power to turn away
Predecessor alone
In bereavement for the journey
That scares me to the bone

I look toward the horizon
Across the desert sea
With only her light to guide me
Here to eternity

1083

Hope that it is not betrayal
Imprisonment of mine
Coping with my loss of life
A harvest of the vine

No longer fit to see the sky
Outside of memory
Under a cross of suffering
Born from heredity

1084

Upon the lawn of yearning
Politics arises
Formed by absolute betrayal
Cloaked in civility

One seeks to escape a beating
By those who were his friends
Across the lawn of betrayal
Where diplomacy dies

1085

Above the trees, the Harvest Moon
To sing my heart a happy tune
From the October sky

A sacred journey through the night
Joy and happiness in my sight
Her blessings, by and bye!

237th Assembly

1086

Roll around in the grass, harlot

Spread your sex to the ground—

To the air

Smile, laugh until you can't breathe

Then lie still and die

1087

Little girls can play with boys too
And not always the other way
Sin can manifest itself early
From the heart of a little girl

Not every prostitute or loose woman
Was molested or abused
There are some who were prodigiously amorous
From the beginning

1088

There are stories I have to tell
No one to hear
Parables inspired by pain
Ordered by Him

My heart is good for the chickens
Their mouths to feed
Trouble rises when I see them
To scratch and claw

Crushed by neverending failure
Time and again
Wishing to have never been born
Dusk until dawn

1089

Though I detest manual labour
As it stands to reason
God blesses those who endure it
In the harvest season

Bread earned by the sweat of the brow
Is unfreely given
Bread from Heaven as manna snow
Unflavored bittersweet

238th Assembly

1090

The chamber where I was buried
Is emptier the room
Now I shall leave it far behind
My former grave and tomb

Adrift the autumnal night breeze
To where the prairie, soon
A spirit walks the Potter's Field
Beneath the Harvest Moon

Farewell to thine sarcophagus
To thy new glory home
Awake, thou autumnal night breeze!
Where I may live to roam!

1091

Heroic bent is delusion
In the palace of the confused
Black armour is no protection
Nor are the yellow eyes

1092

Above the tree line, the star moves
In the morning day
Announce the start of future work
Trouble on the way

Above the tree line, the star moves
In the evening day
Announce the end of future work
Trouble gone away

1093

A knock at my door has no sound
Not done to be mean
Of those who wander to and fro
No wish to be seen

Up my walk is the torch bearer
Black eyes--burning green
With Hellish coals to warm the hearth
No mercy to glean

Behold, the fire man cometh hence
Absence of the Queen
In the dawn of the new abode
Mansion house pristine

1094

Imprisoned by a solemn rain
With splashes all about
Drowned in a world of busywork
Set up by the elite

239th Assembly

1095

I would take him down to the floor

The young man thought of him

Learning he was the Thunder Man

Killer of the woman

1096

I wouldn't build a house to it
But I will die by it
The music of my life is fear
The melody is pain

Even away from the gravesite
I can still feel the tomb

1097

The death of Indian Summer
Touches mist to my skin
After the harvest yield is stored
When dark has come again

On my stroll through the morning dew
Recalling where I've been
The darkened woods border my world
A place for hiding in

1098

She doused the lights and went to sleep
In her coffin bed
Those who knew her wondered when
She would rest 'til dead

There was a time when suitors came
Into her room she led
To savor the terror in their eyes
When they saw the coffin bed

They choked a scream and tore away
Far from her house, they fled
Deep in the Carolina woods
She sleeps in her coffin bed

240th Assembly

1099

The golden iris is the key
Future prosperity
Although no living eyes can see
Solemn predestiny

Is thunder in a November rain?
Awake ye muses three!
Truth is the alabastar horse
In the mud industry

The golden iris is the key
Their sensibility
Will be dashed against a rock bed
And cast into the sea

1100

Your evil voice is very strong
Said poetry to me
Is it ugly, I said to her
She replied, "it can be"

Her beauty speaks the voice of God
Though never on her own
A flower garden preordained
And tended to alone

1101

Where the wind blows
Is where I wish to be
Across the prairie—through the trees
Paradise to see

Away the burden of this life
Desire to be free

1102

My only freedom is the word
That none may ever see
For my coffin is above ground
Awaiting patiently

But I ride the winds on the word
Of Divine Prophecy
To render warning to the world
Of eschatology

241st Assembly

1103

The Portrait is a source of pain
Crumbling me into dust again
With no relief to give
A treasure languished in the dirt
To render forth a Tree of Hurt
And no reason to live

1104

"Success will find you when you're ready"
They have been known to say
Schoolyard—boardroom—cemetery
Their own appointed way

1105

Lust and sin are conceived in some
Snakes in their mother's womb
There, it grows and transforms itself
Exploding from its tomb

Writhing into the world around
Venom encased in doom
Slithered among the populace
To poison and consume

1106

Congratulations from the angel
For saving the little girl's life
Infatuation from the angel
For a bright moment in this life

Ghosts from the past stroll the gray line
Announced by the gift of gab
While the little girl and me look on
In the cavern of the dead

Black and gray around us
At the crosswalk of the spirits
One room looks "bready", she said
The other sings too much music

These golden pills are poison
Waiting to do the deed
To pass away in a choking noise
Silently in need

242nd Assembly

1107

To bid farewell to clarity
The pleasure that she gives
Rhythm impedes inspiration
Rhyme is where trouble lives
To stroll the fields of mystery
Profoundly flowers bloom
Seeking first the Kingdom of God
No others in the room
To bid farewell to clarity
Under a cloud of doom
Giving heed to His voice alone—

As well Hers to resume.

1108

Cease and desist your common law
You're only fooling yourselves
Be not deceived—God is not mocked
For whatsoever a man soweth
That shall he also reap

It is unholy in the eyes of God—
A union unblessed

1109

The road ahead is a might boisterous
Boyful luck all around
Jennifer Anniston loves Brad Pitt
Music to the ground

Happy feelings are real enough
In the cabin of the Sheen
They won't let us live in peace
With nothing in between

Lester, you're a dingbat
Go home to watch in peace
Old Navy is come a calling
In red performance fleece

I know you would like to "Pennsylvania"
Lets move and travel on
On the eve of the fire rain
And blood encrusted dawn

1110

Now Fungalooga is at hand
And she is dressed to kill
Come to steal your sanity
Against your fervent will

No baker's dozen here, slim
Jet planes fly with skill
High above the mountains
And every lonely hill

243rd Assembly

1111

We could use a bum to gather the wood
Said the wealthy 'round the fire
They'll do anything we say
With little money for hire

A rich boy strolls the Garden Lawn
In a fog mist of gray
Remembering the bum he threw off his property
In the glow of the Evening Day

1112

A stroke and heart attack together
Threaten a call
Waking me up in a cold sweat
Wondering when

Manners justify limitations
Lust and sin
Blow bubblegum wishes to your past
Like Gunga Din

Nifty noodles in the pot
Now stirring up
Take them quicky when they're done
His fervent cup

1113

In the glow of melancholy blue
The Moon has turned to blood
Above the white cloud in motion
By the symbol of the Cross

The cloude glides across the sky
On an upward move
High enough for all to see
Before it goes away

1114

I see every new clock with hatred
Turning of dawn
Eyes opened into the cold
An unwelcome breath

In preparation for marriage
A new place to go
Stroll the grieving land in new cloth
Eyes of desire

To gather positivity
The ultimate goal
Admiration from the heart of them
Kisses from their soul

244th Assembly

1115

A son afraid of his father
Not a good thing to see
Afraid to speak when spoken to
Cowering fearfully

What is a poor father to do
When these conditions lie
Knowing that the sound of his voice
Could cause his son to cry?

1116

Phasing into another world
Where travelers live to dream
Technology from the future
Brings pain and misery

Stifling the hidden growth of trees
Crushed under stainless steel
To show that Earth has gone away
Lost among the stars

Voices speak of what once was
As well what might have been
While other crews get the glory
What Peter Jennings said

1117

An empty and meaningless life
Nowhere I wish to stay
Trapped inside a lonely prison
Day after every day

1118

Every morning I wake up
In the presence of God
Hoping to walk arm and arm with him
But by the noon hour—

Though I see him afar off
Shining brightly like a star
I long to feel the warmth from this light
But I cannot

So, I walk on—comforted by what I see
Guided by the starlight
Knowing that the heat of a star—
Is not given

245th Assembly

1119

Removing the shells intrepidly
To see what is underneath
Lobster tails with butter
Cannot alleviate the pain

1120

Filled with melancholy dreaming
My night upon the waves
Warnings blowing in the storm
Of future sorrow

Lightning pearls from the clouds
Beads of white marble
Black markings in the clouds are omens
Of the devil's touch

A thunderstorm of change
Blows the eternal sea
Splashing me with warnings
Of Melancholy Bay

1121

Dining a la carte with the dead
Solutions arise
While the ancestry sits in grief
For years come and gone

On a stroll through the new abode
Filth is clearly seen
Washed away by a miracle
Appears then the black

Splashing the new identity
Pains of liquid blue
As the dinner hour beckons
Dining with the dead

1122

The sign appears in the night clouds
Of the second coming
On our stroll with the unworthy elite
After worship has failed again

Some answer the Earthly call
To a mountain of prosperity
Reaching out to others—
To lure them into despair

The elite guide us into the city
After the sign has faded
Doing a deed of double dealing
In the dark of night

Trapped in the heart of the city
Where two legged monsters rule
Trying hard to escape the axe
Weilded in Hellish tones

Piety sees the angel sign
Smiling of its beauty
With no connection to those beneath them
Nor the Giver of the Sign

On our stroll though the Grieving Land
Touched by those in power
Crushed by the weight of their lies
When they vanish into night

246th Assembly

1123

Laugh in Laughterland sweetly
Through a brilliant disguise
It hurts too much to travel on
Although we must surmise—

Purpose is found where none is said
Ineptitude will flash
Revealing it is not ourselves
But through the Hand of God

Images plague to deliver
Like footprints in the sand
With no choice but to walk with Him
Across the Grieving Land

1124

Marshall Dillon is a reflection
Of the modern need
To triumph good over evil
Now, a dying breed

Modernity worships Carnality
And every type of sin
With no knowledge of the afterlife
The Hell they're going in

1125

Have I been embalmed, I asked
On my funeral's eve
So I would not reawaken
And cause her soul to grieve

In the Church of the Living Dead
Corpses roam about
To moan and groan their calling
Pained by what took them out

Reanimation turns them green
Their eyes may pop in their head
While they endure Hellish resurrection
In the Church of the Living Dead

1126

To stroll the field with an angel
A solemn wish for hiding in
Watching the denizens around us
Go suffering to and fro

Always on the edge of pain
In the shadow of the steeple
Unaware that all their agony
Was caused by other people

On my stroll with the angel
On the living side of war
The bombs burst a world away
At the apocalyptic shore

247th Assembly

1127

How many billions of empty gun shells
Populate the fields
Enough to build a golden tower
That would stretch from here to heaven

Rising high among the clouds
Monument to our fate

1128

Blackbird in the snow
Shivering in the cold
Ill concerned for where to go
But hungry for a meal

Blackbird in the snow
Lying dead in the cold

1129

Hypocrisy is a disease
Plaguing the new world
Purveying all types of evil
In secret

The cure for it lies hidden well
Under the coffin lid
Revealed to them who lie beneath
In secret

1130

Away from formality!

All ye who require clarity—

Selection is here!

Words gathered as a bouquet of wildflowers

Every color shape and size

Placed together—

As only they see fit to go

Away from clarity!

Her tired beauty grows wearisome

Lyricism beckons a call

Not from beyond the sea—

Or the clouds

Or the grave

Nor even the heart

Clarity screams as I reject her

As I send her to the woods to live—

To be lost forever

248th Assembly

1131

Longfellow's rhyme will live forever
No need to wish I was dead
"There was a little girl, who had a little curl
Right in the middle of her forehead"

Clarity is a hundredfold
Come back to me from the wood
Gripping me in such a violent hold
I wouldn't escape if I could

"There was a little girl, who had a little curl
Right in the middle of her forehead"
Longfellow's rhyme will live forever
No need to wish I was dead

1132

On the road to Madison, West Virginia
Her shoes are caked with clay
By the path through the Adam Wood
Before a rainy day

Clouds gather above our journey
Along the country road
Until we arrive our destination
Where the children cannot see

Rising high above the road
Our path to prosperity
Trees go swaying in the breeze
Above our feet of clay

Arriving our destination
In hopes to be left alone
Grieving for our country road
To come and take us home

1133

Bobwhites sing to the aliens
"Go in through the door!"
But the aliens take their appointed way
The bedroom window instead

In the morning light—the children scream
At the figure in the hall
As the red lights come through the window
Without breaking it at all

1134

Whose bikini will die soon—
In the roaring ocean waves?
Where will the current pull their body
To the depth of the sounding sea?

This wind blows a mighty hand
In the ocean spray
To take the bikini clad woman
To her death

In the roar of the crashing waves
The current reaches out
To steal her life away

249th Assembly

1135

Daily, weekly, monthly, yearly
A wife vexes the nerve
More than she soothes them, everly
Burning the astral curve

Dearest heart, an help meet for him
Earning what he'll deserve

1136

Banded clouds swim the ocean sky
Turning of the blue
Toward a lavender evening time
A star comes out to play

High above the tree line forest
Amber dissolves to gray
Bands of orange vanishing
My loneliness away

1137

Rossini on the modern stage
Those who love opera and no
Rosina for two hundred years
A barber named Figaro

A divinely inspired overture
Improper to Aureliano
Touching the Elizabethan tongue
At the summit mount, Bel Canto

1138

I watched a droplet go down a window
Gleaming in the sun
The ladybug left by its wake—
Pity the chosen one!

The autumn blows a humid breeze
In the November Summer
To lull in false security
Before the evening comes

250th Assembly

1139

My prayer to the night cloud
Is "Do not hide my star"
It flickers dangerously—
On the edge of going out
It blinks precariously—
To threaten Beauty's Demise

As I pray to the looming night cloud
"Do not hide my star"
Let my star live, that I may see it shine—
Another hour—
Another minute—
Another second in the timeline

Oh Heavenly Father—
I beseech thee!
Rebuke the hands of the Night Cloud
And let me see my star again!

1140

O Glory, O Blessed Day!
O glorious, Heavenly reprieve
When I see the glimpse of my star again!
Shining brightly in the mist—
Behind the feeble life of the cloude
That came to steal this light from me

I know that behind the gray
In the looming black it brings,
My star shines in beauty
In power—
In glory—
By the almighty hand of God

1141

The half-dollar angel sang in tune
"You're too good to stop"
Confections promise sustenance in sweet
As the barrier threatens to fall

A trip through the maze of learning
Past old perversions unknown
Reveals a way lost to consciousness
Dependant upon the Lord

251st Assembly

1142

A gold cloth decorates the table
Where a Thanksgiving feast will live
Souls roaming the room in happiness
Joyful among the dead

From the island sails the simple minded
By beauty's heart and soul
With nothing but kindness to give
Tormented by the dead

Wisdom hides in antiquity
At the ancestry's House of Clay
Trees blossom crimson petals and blue
In the garden of the dead

Fear seeks to hide from memory
Creeping down the road
Trying to hide behind the locked door
In the chamber of the dead

Elizabethan VIII

False hope blares a trumpet sound
To the disillusioned
Still a daydream believer—
On the morning of the dead

1143

Now comes the November wind
To steal the leaves from every tree
Under skies of autumn blue
Every colored leaf is blown

1144

It took her ten years to get ready
To run the race in the snow
Though she was miles and days behind
She gathered herself up to go

In the forest of prosperity
Squirrels the girth of dogs
Her journey leads to nowhere
At the base of Forest Hill

At Broken Bridge Crossing
A miracle occurs
Getting her to the other side
On her trip to Prairie Green

After ten years of waiting
To run the race in the snow
Arriving her destination
With nowhere else to go

1145

Two souls named Hate and Vengeance
From their house of doom
Send cruelties to the atmosphere
Directed towards my room

A core of venom in their hearts
Lack of forgiveness to the Moon
More than lack of tolerance
Radiates a poisoned tune

Years have not softened their resolve
Hearts of Judgment and Doom
Having no wish for civility
But rather my death and tomb

252nd Assembly

1146

From the learning hall to the horizon
Outside the open door
Feathers flocked in certain death
Waiting to come in

Perverse communications
Shocking numbers abroad
Accursed illuminations
Behind doors of every home

God shields mankind from nature
His imminent demise
Could tether as a feathered flock
In Tranquility's disguise

1147

Strumenize yourselves all you want
Chocolate sweets to thine hearts content
Butter reflects casual caking, too
Down subdivezened way

Colts toss the ball in ignorance
Delayed to carry on
Grasses grow on Harmony's Field
In the dawning of the day

Night fit for me in Harmin's Divine
A tight fit for me in Charm's Divine
Nevercream wishes in candies sweet
Silken babes alarm sublime

Golden necklaces outright
Dropped from Heavens Kiss
Cropped by friendships chosen "Oprah"
In craving to get in

What's meant to be will happen
And crowned queen of the ball
Without worries first at all
By the Chiming of the Whistle Train

1148

Deep meditation for her verse
Deep medication would be worse
Nothing for us to hear!

Sweet dedication should be first
Complete education could be the worst
Nothing for us is here!

1149

Transported by the living
Over the prairie green
Seeing ghosts from 1939
Conjured by Mervin Leroy

David Moab is the subject
Spoken by the money maker
Put on this earth to spin yarn
For capital gain

Precariously over the countryside
By an uneasy repose
Phantoms from 1939
Waiting for me to die

253rd Assembly

1150

Raptors dine uneasy prey
In the theatre of the mind
Rachnids threaten deadly unfurling
Limbs too terrible to see

Demons threaten without fail
A feast of humanity
Unable to penetrate the barrier
Which is the power of Him

1151

The morning sun lights my eye
In a corner of the room
Though her “tippet” be only “tulle”
And that rightly soon

Await the turning of the day
To sing a happy tune

1152

A ghost roams the Halls of Acre
To terrify our souls to ashe
When a blackened hand appears in the air
I take hold of it and pull

The hand pulls away from me
Vanishing out of sight
While little Emily roams the halls in fear
Trembling for the Ghost of Acre

1153

Ghosts of the deceased are watching
Fair humans in disguise
An accusatory finger
Pointed in their demise

254th Assembly

1154

Racism still permeates society
Though it is kept hidden from view
In the heart of our fervent memory
It waits to disappear forever

1155

Two souls adrift toward one another
Through Debrianna Woods
Chasing the dream of solidarity
But being unable to find it

Hold your claim on forgotton soil
It waits for no one
In the grand scheme of things
Everything matters

Wait for eschatology!
It will devour us all
Don't call her stupid!
The words are like a sledgehammer—
To her spirit

1156

A tree whispers a night breeze
On turning of the North Wind
Beneath colors of the Evening Day
Precedes the coming night

A chill summons Winter's Eve
When Venus shines so bright
To rule Amherst Lake—the call of winter
Where none endeavor to grieve

A tree whispers the night breeze
On turning of Winter's Eve
By the glory of Almighty God
A snowy winter to achieve

1157

When the house is warm on winter's eve
The window invites to be opened
So the Barrier Blessing can be felt
Divine protection from the cold

A brush of winter's icy hand
Roams diligently the skin
Without power to chill the blood
Nor the soul

255th Assembly

1158

A lonely celebration
Hard times come and gone
Of no concern to another soul
Except a party of one

Intruders through the dreary gate
To dance upon my grave

1159

As the noontime train rides clickety clack
A young girl inside talks yickety yack
She clattered like rain—Miss Alma Gazoo
She chattered 'til the train got to Calamazoo

1160

Among the treasure gems she found
Few likely to exceed
That *"success is counted sweetest"*
"By those who ne'er succeed"

Her majesty the Horizon
Queen o'er my dying need
To know what flourisheth her crown
Beyond where I can see

Twenty years in the wilderness
Signs of the times to read
There being only Destiny
And hungry souls to feed

1161

The maestro adds gloom and doom to the world
As almost where my mind would take
To have us afraid of phantom aliens
And dinosaurs never there

Symphonies of colored light
Concertos of worthy sound
Bringing magic into the real world
That destiny has known

I was chosen from a dark field
As a purveyor of truth
Left to fend for myself in gloom
Where dinosaurs rule the earth

The maestro stolls through the train
To where I sit in awe
To shake my hand with diligence
To ask me a question I cannot hear

I know to say “its terrifying”
Concerning this train we ride
Evoking the smile of approval
And laughter for my pride

256th Assembly

1162

If publication were mine
I could not avoid her
She would rest her gentle knocking
Until I answered the door

In the light of the Forest Moon
Her silhouette is gone
To rap a tapping for another
That I may be left alone

1163

On the prairie field with the dead
Fading our plan to naught
Life was a funnier riddle
To the West Virginia boy

In the garden of iniquity
Foolishness abounds
Awaiting the rise of Amherst Lake
Over the prairie green

Pain cares for the grassy field
Tended by the dead
With wicked hands to avoid her
While birds have chirped and fled

1164

Winter twirls a whirlwind of snow
At the foot of the lavender tree
Towering in flowers blooming
Annually in the cold

In the window are the milk boy twins
In their sleeping bed
Wondering if the star will move
Above the winter snow

A tree grows in lavender bloom
In the field of white
Adjacent to one in crimson red
And shrubbery in blue

1165

For 90 days she blindly stood
While her boyfriend kindly stood
In idleness nearby
To make her regret this sylvan scene
Exchanging thoughts too harsh and mean
Endeavoring not to cry

257th Assembly

1166

Tending the lawn at prairie green
Hearts are bravely stationed
None regardless of the past
Others work gravely on

Printed lies still mock
Over Failure's Lawn
The ancestry speaks in riddles
While the dead tend their plots

The will of God is carried out
By human hands
The right tree and the wrong tree
Are both cut down—
With blind enthusiasm

1167

An angry cloud passes overhead
Wishing to cause death to me
Charging to throw a lightning bolt
For my accursed condition

The face of the cloud is hatred
Toward the flesh that is me
Craving to rain the drowning water
To my accursed condition

1168

To take an axe to every property tree

Burning lived wood and glass from view

To see amber fire—clouds unobstructed

A solemn wish to do

1169

Caroline! Oh Caroline!

What blessings dost thou give!

Lips as sweet as cherry wine

Enchanted life to live!

1170

To make a good story from a bad one
Them that spin the yarn
Struggle—in vain against the truth
Of their inspiration

Tapestry upon the harvest loom
Every color and kind
Woven to alleviate the pain
And burdens on the mind

258th Assembly

1171

Fear of a dreadful populace

Their razor teeth and claws

Lions, tigers and bears

Running through my kitchen

A knock at the door is a grizzly bear

Clawing to get in

1172

HG Wells and Steven Spielberg
Partners in a crime
To steal complacency from our hearts
Nearby the end of time

The call of eschatology
By each three-legged "pod"
Echoes the coming Judgment
From the Trinity of God

Three bear witness in heaven
Lord, thy will be done
The Father, Son and Holy Ghost
And yet, these three are one!

1173

A future plan is on the map
Devised the simple and wise
Chitterlings are not on the menu
At the world stage theatre

The sun burns the chosen face
Prompting ingenuity
It creates a refuge in shadow
Where other plans are made

The wise talks to the simple
In the gray chariot of dreams
Neither in the power of autonomy
By the will of the most High

1174

A mountain in the sky
Rises and falls above the city
Slopes of white and brightened glory
Fading into blue

259th Assembly

1175

"Do you want me to beat her"
Said poetry to me
I'll beat her to an inch of her life
If that's what's required of me

I stood idly by, in shock to hear
The poison from poetry's mouth
The same eyes that took Marie Antoinette
And lifted her head away

1176

2:37 is the witching hour
When demons come to play
To frighten you beyond your wits
In the nighttime of the day

1177

The name falls flat on the surface

Born inadequacy

Wishes masquerade as beauty

A love lorn tragedy

1178

The blue rabbit leapt through the clouds
To carve a place in time
Jumping high across the ocean
Leaving his cares behind

The white clouds frame a rabbit blue
Leaping through the bright divine

260th Assembly

1179

A walk with the ancestry reveals
A day of independence
Speaking to them on the miracle
Bestowed to their descendants

Fear rides the train through the forest
In hopes to escape corruption
Unclean symbols mar the journey
No pardon for their interruption

1180

To grow old and die
Is my greatest desire
Verses are the worst
Riches corrupt the soul

Poverty is filth and bondage
Love is a weary goal
The grave is my bestest calling
Would that I could dress to rest!

In silken midnight blue pajamas
Better than my Sunday best!

1181

Heaven and Hell are of little concern
To Paul and Paula Dini
Rather the no tell motel
And what cut and color bikini

Where did the cat go when he died?
Raises a greater frown
Than whether to look up from Grandma's grave
Or whether instead to look down

1182

Yellow skinned beauty—come to me!
Arrest my sensibility
Gaze upon me—brown eyed beauty
Hearken my soul to thee!

261st Assembly

1183

Two beauties roll the color wheels
Across the sea of green
Balls of color in competition
To crown a billiard queen

One in somber eyes that stare
Voluptuousness in the loom
Conquered by a yellow rose
They call the Dutchess of Doom

1184

I write in the cool of the evening
By the light of the mountain moon
Near the waters of a sounding sea
A bright and sounding sea

Far by these shores of mystery
Voices of clarity

1185

Ledda Miza Jay!

Ledda Miza Jay!

O Sweet Lord,

Ledda Miza Jay!

Now, down in old Kentucky
In the Allegheny Woods
There lived a sweet old Granny Ma
Where a crumpled cabin stood

Old granny had a granddaughter
In Maco County Wood
Precious as the April Rain
Arletta Miza Jane

One rainy day in the mountain wood
Sweet old granny died
Miza Jay took up a shovel
And dug the best she could

Elizabethan VIII

She drug ole granny through the forest
As a good ol' grand girl should
Miza Jay buried sweet ol' granny
In their mountain forest wood

Ledda Miza Jay!
Ledda Miza Jay!
O Sweet Lord,
Ledda Miza Jay!

Ledda Miza lived alone
In her cabin by the woods
She cooked and cleaned and grew her crops
The best she ever could

She read her bible every day
To Christ the Lord she prayed
Ledda Miza worked the fields
Til the cool of the evening day

Ledda heard a knock one night
Outside her cabin door
The angel of death called her name and said
"You can't live here anymore"

Its time for us to go now
To that fair and distant shore
To wait for Him 'til Judgment Day
Ledda Miza Jay

Twenty years had went on by
Since old Granny Ma had gone
For twenty years Ledda Miza lived
In her cabin all alone

1186

She rides along in the night town
Whispering a brilliant prayer
A blackened car in silhouette
Placebo on the dare!

262nd Assembly

1187

Drawers open and close in the dark
With no one in the room
Eyes appear in a clay statue
Looking at me

1188

Close encounters of the third kind
Not a movie, but a boy
Who saw the spaceship in his yard
So much bigger than a toy!

1189

Place thine hands upon the keys
See what sounds thy make!
Seek to show thineself approved
For each appointed mistake

Each step brings less certainty
What destined fools are we!
Trying too hard to know the way
To where the cemetery will be

1190

Hell is hotter than a campfire
To roast marshmallows upon
Whole families are there already
In the midst of having fun

If the righteous shall scarcely be saved
Where will the ungodly appear?
Roaming the earthen wilderness
Year after blessed year

263rd Assembly

1191

I saw the end of the world today
Over the eastern barrier in amber sway
Lovejoy is the fire of this earthly dream
From the morning light until the evening day

1192

Don't move, she said
It's the biggest in the land
There's a spider crawling up your leg
That's bigger than my hand!

Don't move, she said
And brushed it to the floor
The biggest spider in the world
Threatened me some more!

1193

Paul McCartney and Jenny Wren
A melody to sing
John Lennon and the widow flower
A tragedy to bring

The lady had a lot to say
Goodbye, Jenny Wren!
When her love had lived and died
In the world they were hiding in

1194

My apologies for using graduation
As an extra syllable in this life
The skin is still tainted
With ketchup and blood

264th Assembly

1195

Michael Landon is on the highway to Heaven
After the disease took his body
When prairie days had come and gone
A better place to be

1196

Only half the wool has been cut
Above anger's evil stare
In the poverty of destitution
By the cold north wind

1197

Silver chalice burdened by the leaven

At the window of Amherst kitchen

Two bright yellow blobs of life

In the leavened field of white

1198

Arrows point toward the North Star
In the cold of winter's eve
Venus cloaked in darkness
At the end of the present age

265th Assembly

1199

She sings "Heartbreaker" in December

To soothe a troubled soul

Mountain girl, I must remember--

Save me from the cold

1200

By the roaring ocean waves
A jealous heart for thee
In a fortnight's anticipation—
At the shore of the sounding sea

1201

A melody crashes baroque dissonance
In the shadow of the Cross
Reprimand the players
For the tragedy of their loss

The ancestry looks in confusion
As beauty crosses the room
With no knowledge of the future
And the losses they'll assume

ABOUT THE AUTHOR

Jonathan Lovejoy is a graduate of the University of North Carolina at Greensboro, with a B.A. in Religious Studies. He currently lives in Winston Salem, North Carolina with his wife, a physical therapist.

For more info on the author's life and career, visit jonathanlovejoy.com.

www.ingramcontent.com/pod-product-compliance
Lightning Source LLC
Chambersburg PA
CBHW060919040426
42445CB00011B/695
* 9 7 8 0 6 9 2 3 1 9 2 5 3 *